Becoming Lilly

By

Lilly Beaumont

All poems and art
By
Lilly Beaumont © 2020

Contents

Dedication		1
Introduction	....	2
Becoming Lilly	....	3
Nemesis	....	7
Self Defense	....	9
Running on Empty	....	11
Q & A	....	13
FRUSTRATED	....	15
EXHAUSTED	....	17
Solitude Creek	....	19
White	....	21
Quiet Desperation	....	23
Cleansing Tears	....	25
Everything Fit	....	27
Moonlight	....	29
Siren	....	31
Almost	....	33
Her	....	35
Her Essence	....	37
Truth	....	39

Dedication:

    To all the older (more mature) women who are entangled in a heterosexual relationship only to realize that they are not so straight. Those who just realized, those in the messy ass middle, and those who are on the other side.

    Thank you, to some very special women who have been walking beside me thru this perilous yet exciting journey. Michelle, who helped me to realize that it was true. Who heard it all and is still my friend. Suzy, who always tells me straight up and has my back. Bev, who took the time to get to know me and who is always so very supportive. Mel and Andi, who graciously donated some photographs to make this book beautiful. And lastly, Mari-Ann, who has had many a conversation with me on the depth of the internal fights we both have had. For reading, commenting, and encouraging me with her creative insights.

    Thank you for giving of your time and your friendships. Words can NOT express how much I appreciate and love you guys!

p.s.

    Ashley. Thank you so much for being my Beta reader. Your input is invaluable. You're amazing!! Thanks for being my friend too!

Introduction:

I've been married for almost 30 years. About 5 years ago I finally admitted to myself that I wasn't so straight. I figured that I was bi-sexual because I was married to a man and had always dated men. I had my share of crushes on both men and women. Never really thought twice about it. Then one day a women caught my attention and made me question how straight I really was. But, OMG, I'm married! I'm christian enough that being gay was not acceptable. So I put those thoughts away. Which worked for a while but honestly was never stuffed far enough down to not bubble back up, occasionally. So I started searching for answers. I could not be the only one that this had happened to. I searched the internet and found that I was not. I was surprised and amazed at the amount of them. I found some articles that led me to a "late in life lesbian story", a blog by Andrea Hewitt. I was lucky to have landed there. There are numerous blogs and support groups. If you search you'll find one that fits you.

    I realized that I was truly mistaken when I thought that admitting I was gay was the hardest decision I was to make. But there is sooo much more. Telling your husband, your family and friends. Breaking up said family. And even trying to live that more authentic life you've been dreaming about.

    This is part of my story. I'm telling it in hopes that it may help someone in knowing that they are not alone.

Becoming Lilly

After years of soul searching
I have ...
Finally discovered that I have a voice
Finally discovered that I have a choice
A choice of who I want to be
A choice of where I want to be

We started this journey together
This journey of self discovery
This journey of self awareness
We walked & searched together
We weathered storms together
And arrived at the same conclusion
Really the only conclusion: I am gay
There was a peace like I've never known

Then I realized that I was in the eye of the storm
I realized, to my horror, that my head
And my heart were at war!

I had made decisions that were
Are right for me.
But... I did NOT see
All the hazards
All the pit falls
That would cause this rift.
Soon I would come to realize
That my head had become
My nemesis

My nemesis, she is not lost
She is troubled
She thinks she can make it
She has made it this far

But the journey is arduous
The trip made more difficult
Not only by the obstacles in the road
But also by the amount of armor
She is now wearing

The sheer weight of her fear
Has slowed her progress
The battles with her demons
Becoming more fierce

After some heartfelt losses
She must stop to rest - to regroup
To find courage,
somewhere in her stores

Then to her delight
She finds an encampment
A group of amazing women, Amazons
Some seasoned, others not so much
But all willing to help
All willing to offer sustenance
Willing to offer words of encouragement
Willing to offer of themselves
Happy to give what they can to help her
continue her journey

And so she rests
She finds comfort in their words
Finds comfort in their presence
She gathers strength and courage

She picks herself up
Takes in hand what they have given her
And begins again

This time with less armor
This time with a renewed spirit
That comes with the knowledge
That she is no longer alone
Finally she can hope
For they have helped her build a bridge
Across the chasm
The chasm that keeps her from her goal
The chasm that keeps her from her heart

Nemesis

I remember the storm
I remember the struggle
I remember the war
I remember the armor
And more

I remember the question
I didn't want to know the answer
I didn't want to be gay
There had to be another way

I had a husband
We had a family
I was Mrs. Wife
I was no longer Lilly

I had lost myself long ago
I had become an extension
Of my husband
Of my family

I was so busy taking care of everyone
That I missed how easily
I had slipped away

But she saw
She made me see
She made me feel things
She made me want things

Of course, I had several problems
I was married. I had a family
I had forgotten
How to take care of myself
How to want a life for myself

How do I reconcile
What my heart wants with
What my heads says?

Self Defense

The war
The one I had with myself daily
The many battles scars I bore
A war for me, for Lilly

I thought that admitting it
Saying it out loud was hard
But it was nothing in comparison
To the shit storm that was coming!

The first battle was telling people
Who to tell?
How are they going to react?
Will they still like me?
Love me?

Then...
Then the shields come
To help you fend off the hurt
To help you defend your decision

The armor that comes when
You start telling people
People you love
People who "love" you

Running on Empty

My head and my heart
Have never been this far apart
The rift so wide and so deep
I am exhausted and want sleep

My head says, no I can't be
My heart says, you are
My head says, I don't want to be
My heart says, you are

We, my head and my heart
Were troubled over this conflict
It was tearing me apart
Was this part of the script?

The back and forth taking its toll
I was running on empty
I had given up my soul
I needed to move gently

Finally, just admitting it
Finally climbing out of the pit
The battle, for now, negated
I was elated

But the euphoria didn't last long
Do I stay or do I leave?
I needed to find where I belonged
I had a new life to weave

So many questions
The more I answered
The more questions I had
What a vicious cycle

I was so overwhelmed
I had no idea where to start
Choices that I'm going to make
Things that I'm about to choose
Choices that may change
my way of life
Things that I may lose

Q & A

I don't know about lesbian life
But I do know about being his wife
I did love him once upon a time
Time has changed the way it is
I have grown into someone different

Once the idea of it took hold
I couldn't close the flood gates
And once you know a truth
You can never take it back
It eats at you
Until you make a change

And so my life changed
The way I thought
The way I looked
The way I felt

There was a freedom in that

FRUSTRATED

There once was a time
When it is what it is
Was acceptable
Was the way it was

Few questions asked
Live life the way you were suppose to
The way society told you to
Find a man, get married, have a family
What it's suppose to be
It is what it is

Then you wake up one morning
Realize what you've been feeling
... is restless
Realize that something is different
Realize that your recurring dreams
have been about loving someone
other than "your man"

Realize that this love you feel ...
is bone deep

Realize that THIS love ...
is the love you've been looking for
your whole life

Realize that this love...
is what "home" feels like

Realize that this all consuming love
... is a woman

How can that be you ask yourself
I'm happily married... to a man
Married some 20 yrs. Have a family

Realize that it is what it is ...
Is no longer acceptable
No longer what will make you happy

And you realize how much
you've come to hate that saying

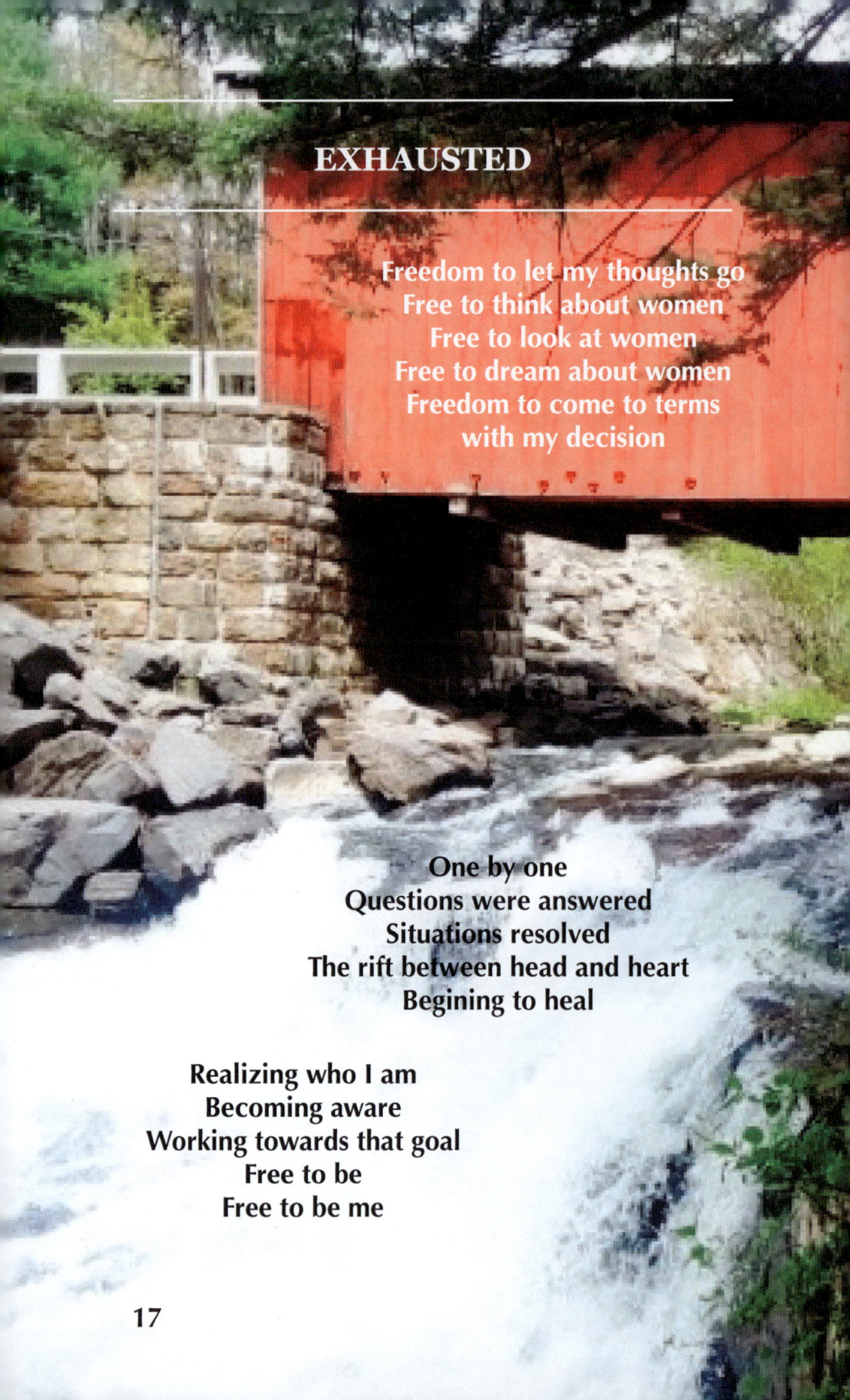

EXHAUSTED

Freedom to let my thoughts go
Free to think about women
Free to look at women
Free to dream about women
Freedom to come to terms
with my decision

One by one
Questions were answered
Situations resolved
The rift between head and heart
Begining to heal

Realizing who I am
Becoming aware
Working towards that goal
Free to be
Free to be me

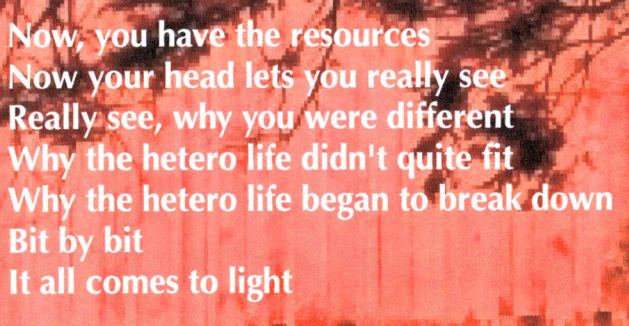

Now, you have the resources
Now your head lets you really see
Really see, why you were different
Why the hetero life didn't quite fit
Why the hetero life began to break down
Bit by bit
It all comes to light

Waves of emotion
Force you to your knees
The sudden release
Of all that was pent up
Descends upon you

Your body is racked with sobs
As wave after wave slams into you
Having no chance to catch your breath
You are forced to ride it out

Time stands still
As grief has it's way with you
And when it's over
You are spent
You are drained

E x h a u s t e d

Solitude Creek

Riding the waves once more
Heading towards some peace
Drifting along without a paddle or an oar
Looking for the world to cease

I need some tranquility
I need some calm
I need some serenity
To work as a balm

Too much in my head
Too much stress
Too much to be said
Too much to express

I find myself on this ride
I make myself disengage
Drifting with the tide
Ready to turn the page

I just need to take a rest
Take a little time to destress
No need to speak
To find what it is that I seek

A trip to Solitude Creek

White

White is the absence of color
Silence the absence of sound
Darkness the absence of light
Please let me expound

Sometimes life is too colorful
And all I want is White
Sometimes life is too loud
And all I want is Silence
Sometimes life is too bright
And all I want is Darkness

Life buries me in the debris
Submerges me in everyday ness
Weighs me down so I cannot flee
Demanding all, Nothing less

I hate the instability
Life's ups and downs
The lack of tranquility
All I want is to shutdown

I know that life is better with color
I know that life is better with sound
I know that life is better with light
Just better all around

But when I'm drowning in the overflow
When I'm trudging thru the mire
When I can't see the rainbow
When things are at their most dire

I have to remind myself that
Eventually the light will come
Eventually the sounds will return
Eventually the color will come back

I have to remind myself to
Reach out my hands
Remind myself that I am not alone
Remind myself to rely on friends

Remind myself that.... Solitude Creek
Is only a place to visit

Quiet Desperation

I'm reaching out in quiet desperation
Weaving words into feelings
Going over them in contemplation
To figure out what I'm concealing

I write them down for others to see
I write them down for others to know
Trying to make them understand me
For it's hard to let my feelings show

The words are not always eloquent
But are chosen with such care
I want to feel that I am relevant
Want someone to understand my despair

I'm not sure that my words can even express
Or if you'll even get my meanings
There are just things that I needed to address
Things that I am feeling

So, if you are reading this verse
Then I've reached out my hand
And maybe I'm ready to converse
Ready to tell you all, my friends

Cleansing Tears

Laying there
Tears all over my face
Feeling like I just got slammed
Emotionally spent
Physically drained

Not yet realizing the significance
Of what I had just experienced
A death of sorts
A cleansing

I wipe my face
Blow my nose
Turn over and lay there
Contemplating

I could not go back to who I was
For she no longer exists
I had to find a way to merge
The old with the new

Because despite the "death"
I still have a life

Everything fit

What I found was amazing
Too good to be true
Everyone thought that I was just phasing
They didn't understand what I was going thru

Everything was right
Everything fit
I found my sexual appetite
And was enjoying every bit

I was loving her feel
I was loving her touch
It seemed so unreal
It seemed like too much

I was a teenager all over again
My body awakened
Unlike with men
All my senses heightened

What a fantastic revelation
To realize that I wanted to
To realize that I could be so brazen
This was all so new

Moonlight

I toss and turn, yet again
Real sleep alluding me
The moonlight shines about the room
As I contemplate what could've woken me

And then I see the most amazing thing
I don't dare move
I can hardly breath
For it is my lover in the moonlight

The moon shines brightly thru the blinds
Allowing me to see
Her sleep tossed hair, wrapped around her face
And flowing down the length of her back

Her lovely face,
peaceful with much needed slumber
The sheet partially thrown back
Allowing me a clear view
Of the graceful curve of her back
And the gentle rise of her beautiful bottom

I manage to pull my eyes away and realize that
It no longer matters what woke me!
Only that I am awake
And have beheld one of the most beautifully
breathtaking sights
My lover in the moonlight!

Siren

I heard your sirens song
And my heart answered it's call
Now our paths have intertwined
And I am lost in the beauty of it all

And now, as with all sailors
Who have heard the sirens call

I AM LOST

Lost in the thought of you
Lost in the want of you

For your words touch me in places
That have long since gone dark
They seep into the cracks
Of my lost and lonely heart

I want only to be on that island with you
To lie within your arms upon the sand
To lose myself in your eyes
To feel your warmth fill my soul

And let the dulcet tones of your voice
Lull me with its sweet musical song

Almost

I wake reaching for her
Feeling her love for me
With my whole being
I can almost see her

Elusive, Ethreal, Beautiful

I close my eyes
I can almost smell her hair
Almost catch her scent in the air
I can almost feel her skin against mine
Almost feel her warmth in my bed
I can almost hear her voice
Almost telling me
Almost saying
"I am here"

I can almost: See her
                Smell her
                 Feel her
                 Hear her ...
                            Almost

Oh how I wish that I could
Reach into my dream
And pull her out
Pull her into my arms
                    Into my bed

Her

Her scent tantalizes my senses
Licks at my desire
Grabs a hold of me with such force
The impact is visceral
She is talking to me
But I hear nothing
I only see her sensual mouth
I watch as her lips curve into a smile
Hmmmm ..... Caught
Her eyes catch mine
And ...

Damn .... DAMN!!

The intensity of the heat in her eyes
Radiates thru my being
And settles .. low
My body is vibrating
With an urgent need
My face begins to flush
She is aware of her affect on me

She smiles again and leans towards me
Her breast brush against mine
My heart beats hard and fast

Her face comes towards me
I am rooted to the spot
Afraid to move

As she moves closer
Her hand steadies on my forearm
Her breasts are against me now
My heart jackhammers
I know that she can feel it too

Her head next to mine
I can smell her hair
I close my eyes
The better to smell, feel

I can feel her warm breath on my neck
It sends shivers down my back

She whispers in my ear
"I'm ready"

Her Essence

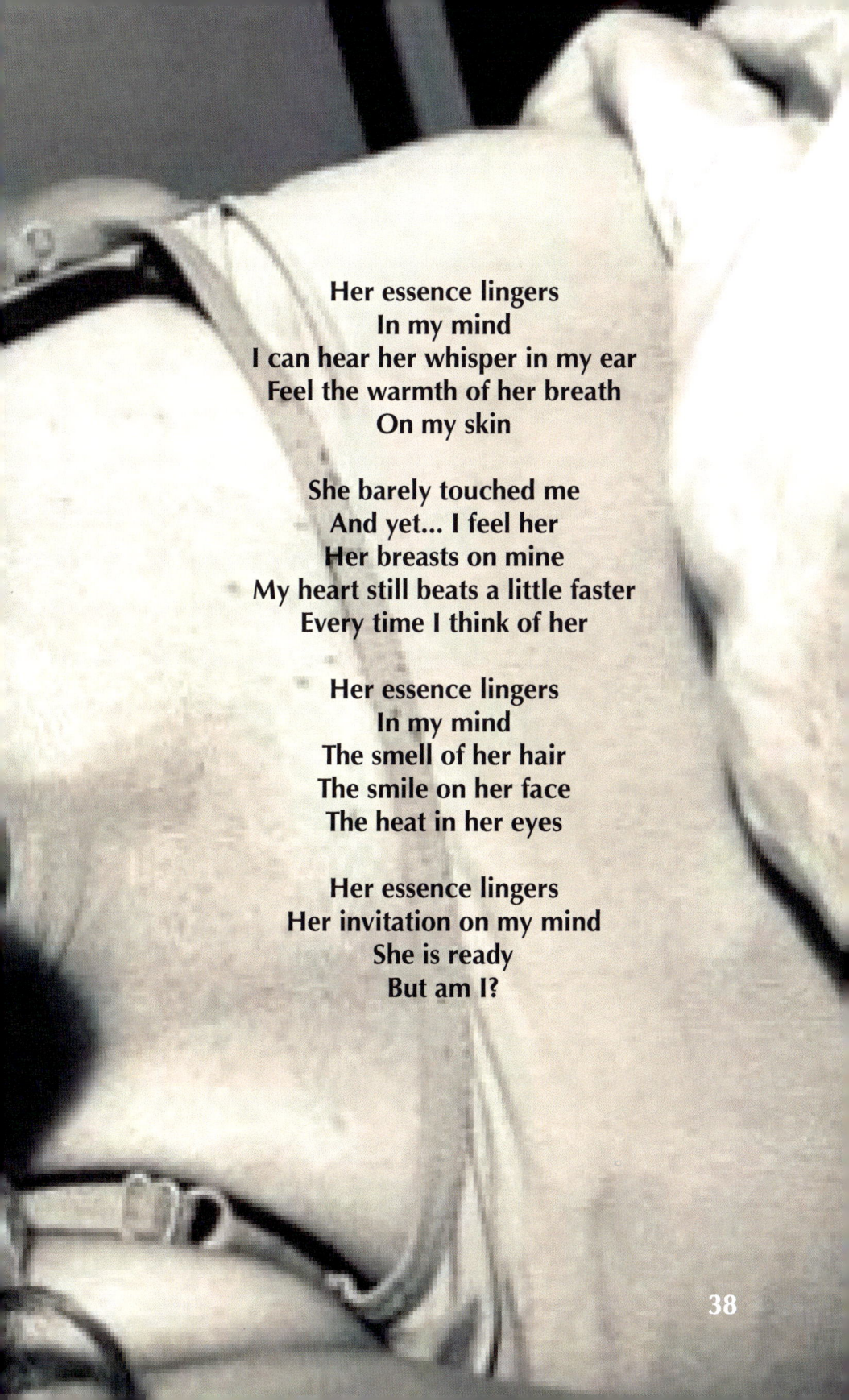

Her essence lingers
In my mind
I can hear her whisper in my ear
Feel the warmth of her breath
On my skin

She barely touched me
And yet... I feel her
Her breasts on mine
My heart still beats a little faster
Every time I think of her

Her essence lingers
In my mind
The smell of her hair
The smile on her face
The heat in her eyes

Her essence lingers
Her invitation on my mind
She is ready
But am I?

Truth

I am Lilly

Listening to the silence
Waiting for you to speak
Waiting for some guidance
To fix the chaos that you've wreaked

Since your "death" I've been a mess
Been lost without a purpose
Trying to move forward without success
Living in the darkness

I ran towards my new life
Like my feet had wings
Shedding people, places
And all sorts of things

I wanted to start fresh, all new
No time for hesitating
No time to undo
No time for waiting

I ran straight into her
I jumped in with both feet
Things went by in a blur
All of a sudden I felt complete

I found what I had been looking for
I found home
I knew this truth to my core
I was searching no more

I am a lesbian

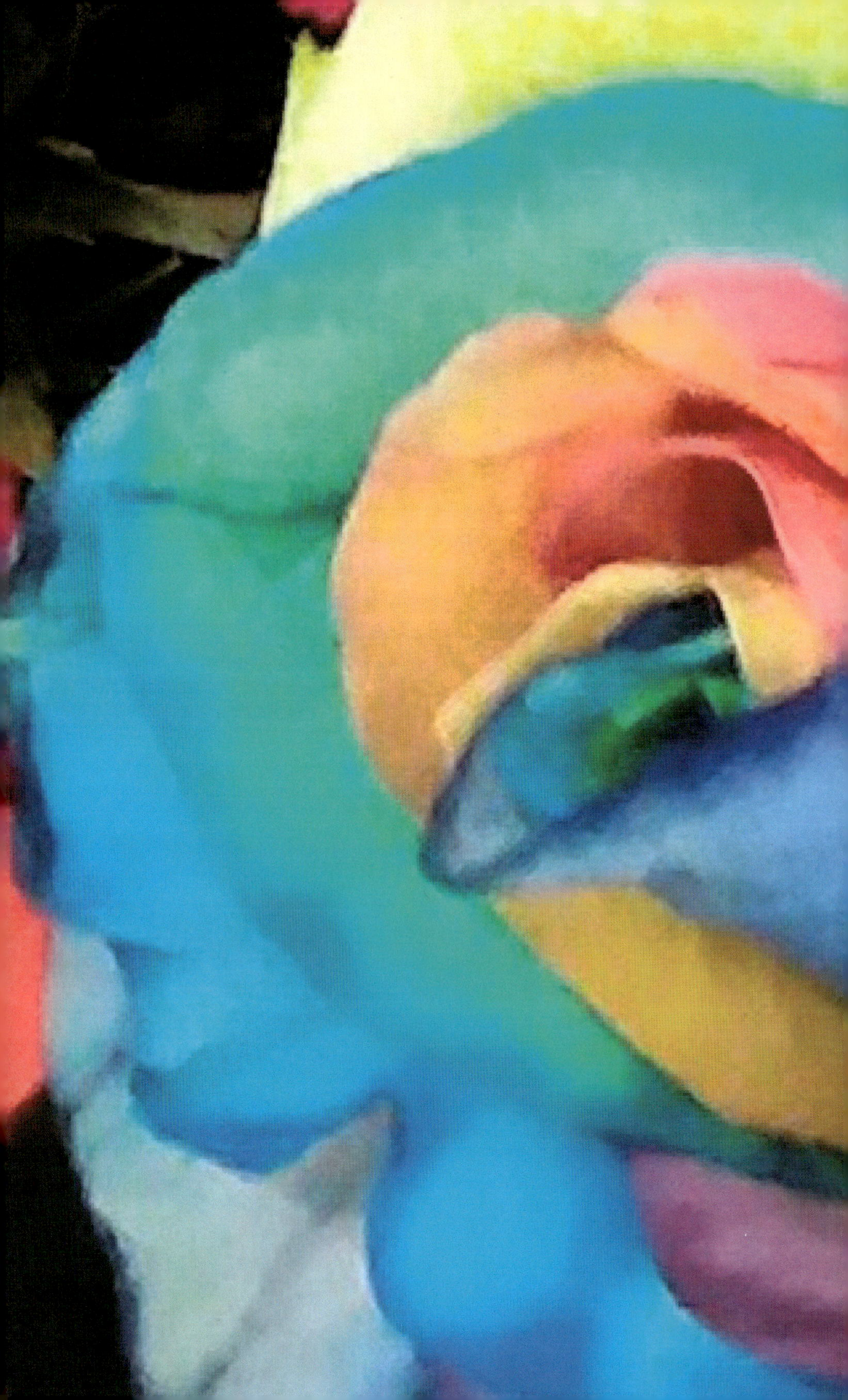

To be continued …

Printed in Great Britain
by Amazon